We Learn About Mass
Second Edition

Teaching Edition

Text by **Gerard Moore**
with additional material by Jean Marie Hiesberger

Cover Illustration by **Jim Burrows**
Interior Illustrations by **Dorothy Woodward,** RSJ

Handbook for Teachers and Catechists

LTP
LITURGY
TRAINING
PUBLICATIONS

Nihil Obstat
Very Reverend Daniel A. Smilanic, JCD
Vicar for Canonical Services
Archdiocese of Chicago
May 5, 2011

Imprimatur
Reverend Monsignor John F. Canary, STL, DMIN
Vicar General
Archdiocese of Chicago
May 5, 2011

Additional material for this teaching edition was written by Jean Marie Hiesberger. The material on pages 3 and 17 was written by Corinna Laughlin and LTP editorial.

WE LEARN ABOUT MASS, SECOND EDITION, TEACHING EDITION © 2011 Archdiocese of Chicago: Liturgy Training Publications, 3949 South Racine Avenue, Chicago IL 60609; 1-800-933-1800, fax 1-800-933-7094, e-mail: orders@ltp.org. All rights reserved. See our Web site at www.LTP.org.

Cover art by Jim Burrows; children's edition illustrations by Dorothy Woodward, RSJ.

ISBN: 978-1-61671-035-4

EWLAMT2

Printed in the United States of America.

Table of Contents

Introduction

The Children's Edition

From the Editor: *To help facilitate your teaching, the children's version of this book is reproduced on the pages within.*

The celebration of Mass, which is also called the celebration of Eucharist, is very important.

We come to Mass to praise God and give thanks for all of the blessings we have received. At Mass we are nourished by God's word and by Eucharist. During Mass we pray for ourselves and for all the needs of our world. We leave Mass with renewed energy to love our brothers and sisters.

At Mass we are all participants: there is no place for spectators! Everyone's participation is important. We all have our specific roles. We dialogue with the priest and pray aloud with the whole congregation. We participate by listening attentively as the word of God is read aloud and explained. In Holy Communion we eat and drink of the Body and Blood of Christ. We sing psalms and hymns and songs. Some of us minister as readers or as singers; others may take part in the procession of gifts or help as altar servers. Some may assist the priest and deacon to distribute Holy Communion.

This book has been written to help you understand more about Mass, and how you participate in it. You will learn the prayers and responses you say out loud, when to stand, to sit, and to kneel, and some of the other actions that are part of Mass.

—Gerard Moore

The Teaching Edition

Welcome to this Teaching Edition

It is a privilege to have the opportunity to help a child learn about Mass. Contained in these pages are tools to help you grow in your understanding of Eucharist in order to better assist a child or group of children to also grow in this way. The more any of us know about this sacred tradition of Mass, the deeper we are able to enter into its celebration. Eucharist is the source and summit of our faith. It is that sacrament to which we bring our life with its joys and sorrows, failures and accomplishments, and put it all in the hands of the Lord. In return, we receive nourishment and strength and are challenged to go forth to more fully love and serve the Lord.

Organization

You will notice that there are always the same three sections to these marginal notes. Each section corresponds directly to the respective page in the children's book. The first section is for you, the adult. It is called "For Teachers and Catechists." The next part offers suggestions for helping children in the second and third grades comprehend and integrate the material. Finally, there are notes for using the booklet with children at about the fourth- and fifth-grade levels. Obviously, you should take the ideas from these last two sections and adapt them to your situation and to the child's maturity level, since some children may not fit neatly into the age category given.

The important notes "For Teachers and Catechists" provide a very brief explanation of that particular part of Mass. It is very important to read and prayerfully reflect on this section each time. Preferably, do this well in advance of any conversation with the child. Never simply skip to doing the children's activities without having had reviewed this material for yourself. Typically, the notes on a given page will describe what we do and why we do it, and how we are to participate in this specific part of the liturgy. Sometimes interesting history or theological background is provided. This information enhances our ability to connect and also gives helpful background to explain what is happening to the children, especially older children. The notes also offer insights about the roles and expectations for everyone involved. Mass is many things, but one thing it is not is private prayer. Yet, sometimes we may not be clear about how that is true and how we can best participate to make it the community prayer Christ gave to us. Learning about Mass is too important a subject, too central a part of our faith, not to take such reflection seriously.

If you are a parent or an adult using this in the family setting, you may not view yourself as a catechist. Please know that you absolutely *are* a catechist! You teach about your faith by what you say and don't say to others, by what you do and don't do in your daily life, by your service, the example of your prayer, and by talking about faith. Certainly the fact that you are spending time with a child on this sacred topic says that you are a catechist.

I hope you will enjoy this experience of catechizing about Mass and that you will learn from it also. If those things are happening, it is sure also to be a rich and worthwhile experience for the children. What greater gift can you give them than to open the door to a deeper spiritual experience of celebrating Eucharist, the Holy Mass!

—Jean Marie Hiesberger

① Introductory Rites

For Teachers and Catechists

How we prepare for something tells us how important it is to us. Think about a significant event or occasion in your life. Perhaps it is a party or a graduation or a special meal, or maybe it is a gathering with friends. We remember the last occasion like this, who was there, and who might be there this time. Whatever the event, if it is important, we think about it beforehand and we do whatever is necessary to see that we are prepared for it.

Recalling these kinds of things helps us reflect on how important Eucharist is for us.

How does it compare with other gatherings in our life? Just as we prepare for other things, we need to pay attention to making the transition from our ordinary daily life to this most important time and place. Developing the habit of preparing for Mass is a valuable one for children to learn and develop at a young age. Helping them to see the celebration of Mass as important and worthy of preparation is a gift they can carry with them through life.

For Second and Third Graders

Let the children name for you some of the important events they go to in their lives: birthday parties, school plays, sports events, movies, Thanksgiving or Christmas dinners, etc. List each one as it is named. Have them recall all the different things they do to get ready to attend. List those under the event. Let them explain their reasons. Make the connection for them of how important the Mass is, too. Write the words "Sunday Mass" and list all their ideas for how to get ready for Mass. Let each child choose one thing they will do to prepare for Sunday Mass this week and name it aloud.

For Fourth and Fifth Graders

In small groups let the students choose a special celebration with a meal. Brainstorm all they might do to prepare to attend. Share their lists with the whole group. Ask them to imagine they have been invited to a special celebration and Jesus Christ will be there. Imagine together what they would do to prepare themselves. Point out that Christ is present at every Mass. He is present in the priest, the scripture readings, the consecrated bread and wine, and the assembly. Now brainstorm with the whole group about how they can best prepare to participate in the Sunday Mass this week.

① Introductory Rites

The Sunday Mass begins with a number of steps.

The first step occurs when we enter the church, gathering together as Christ's sisters and brothers. From the time we leave home we should be preparing our minds and hearts to come together to meet the Lord.

Draw a picture of yourself leaving home to come to Mass.

ACTIVITY

For Teachers and Catechists

In our Catholic tradition we have many different kinds of prayer. Some are private prayers and some are community prayers. Mass is the supreme community prayer. We sing and say our prayers together. The priest includes us in the prayers he prays in the name of the community. In addition to participating fully, we can help make this a community celebration by including other people with simple human gestures as we enter the church. From the very beginning of entering the church, we can acknowledge others. We say "hello" to them as we enter the church. We want to especially notice people who may be there alone or who may be strangers or newcomers. A wave, a handshake, a smile—whatever is comfortable for us—is an important gesture that says, "We are here together. This is a community celebration, not my private prayer."

For Second and Third Graders

Just as we imagined how to prepare for any special occasion, recall what we do when we arrive at a special celebration. Emphasize greeting each other, smiling prior to entering the church, and showing that we are happy to be there together. This is what we do as we enter the church for Mass, also. Once in our place, we prepare by quietly remembering what we have come to do at Mass. After discussing these two actions with the children, let them fold a paper and illustrate both actions: welcoming each other and quietly preparing to participate.

For Fourth and Fifth Graders

Talk with the students about the differences between private prayer and community prayer. Help them appreciate the importance of Mass as community prayer. Review how we join together in words, songs, gestures, silence, and eating at Mass. Suggest how we symbolize that belief as we enter the church. Review the importance of preparing before Mass begins by thinking in our hearts about why we are here and how we will celebrate. Brainstorm together on the importance of both kinds of preparation and their differences.

- Have your students do the activity on page 2 in the children's edition.

ACTIVITY:

What is the best way to prepare for Mass once we have entered the church?

(Write your answer below, and share it with others.)

2

For Teachers and Catechists

The liturgy begins with the Entrance Procession. This procession completes the gathering of God's people, which has already begun as the faithful have arrived at the church and have taken their seats for the celebration of Mass. The procession—led by the cross-bearer (or, sometimes the thurifer, the one with the incense)—suggests the procession of God's people through history, led by Jesus on a journey leading to the heavenly city. The procession is orderly, with servers, lectors, deacons, and priests taking their particular place according to their particular role. The procession should remind us of the variety of gifts that the community brings to the celebration of the liturgy.

The procession is not just about those involved—the priest(s), deacon(s), lector(s), server(s), and other ministers. it is about our moving toward a life in Christ. It is important that the procession moves through the church and among those gathered together for worship. It is important that those in the procession sing the Entrance chant with those gathered for worship. Remind your students that we are all pilgrim people. We are on a holy journey together. The procession symbolizes that holy journey. The Entrance Procession is the first sign of our communal worship.

For Second and Third Graders

Ask your students the following:

- When have you seen a procession? What was it for? Was it in church? Did it take place somewhere else? Where?

- Who took part in the procession?

- Were the people in the procession holding something? What were they holding?

- Why was the procession important?

- Think about the Mass. Why do you think we process at Mass?

For Fourth and Fifth Graders

Ask your students the following:

- What happens during the Entrance Procession at Mass?

- Who takes part in the procession?

- Are the people in the procession holding something? What are they holding?

- What are we doing while the ministers are processing?

- What do you think a procession means? Why is it important for worship?

The second step is when the priest and ministers enter in a procession. There is always a cross. Usually there are candles. Sometimes there is a minister carrying the Book of the Gospels, and at other times incense.

The ministers enter the sanctuary at the front of the church, and the priest and deacon kiss the altar out of respect. Sometimes they incense the altar and the cross. During the procession we all stand and sing the Entrance Chant. Singing unites us and helps us enter into the Mass.

The Sign of the Cross and The Greeting

For Teachers and Catechists

As Mass begins, we make the Sign of the Cross. We start and end our celebration with this important sign of our faith. The Sign of the Cross is laden with meaning and symbolism. We pray in the name of the Trinity, professing our faith in the Father, the Son, and the Holy Spirit. This is an act of faith as well as a reminder to ourselves that all we do is grounded in the three persons in one God. The Sign of the Cross is a sign of the most perfect act of love, Christ's death on the cross for our salvation. There is no greater love than this. We also make the Sign of the Cross to ask God to bless us. We touch our head, remembering that we are blessed in our mind. We touch our shoulders and heart, remembering that we are blessed in all of our being, and in this gesture, we ask God to continue to bless us. Next, we offer the ancient blessing to each other. We respond to the priest's greeting and listen attentively to his invitation to enter into the most important celebration of our Catholic faith.

For Second and Third Graders

Without any introduction, slowly make the Sign of the Cross, saying the words clearly. Then ask the children to join you in doing it again. Talk about the name, "Sign of the Cross." Hold up a cross or crucifix and make the connection between it and the sign you just made. Review the words with them, stressing their meaning and importance. Remind them that we begin and end all our prayers this way, especially Mass. Remind them of the prayer–response: "The Lord be with you." "And with your spirit." Talk about the meaning of this and how we begin every Mass this way. Have the children stand with a partner and say this prayer and response. Remind them to notice these prayers on Sunday at the beginning of Mass.

For Fourth and Fifth Graders

Review with the children both the Sign of the Cross and greeting with which we begin every Mass. Focus on their meaning and the reasons why they are so appropriate and symbolic here at the start of the liturgy. Divide into small groups and let each group list all the ways we are blessed in our mind, heart, and all our being. Encourage them to name ways we show this in our daily life.

Close by having each child stand and pray the Sign of the Cross with confidence, knowing that they are blessed.

- Have your students do the activity on page 4 in the children's edition.

The Sign of the Cross

The priest makes the Sign of the Cross.

He says: *In the name of the* _____ , *and of the* _____ , *and of the* _____ _____ .

We respond: *A* _____ .

> ### ACTIVITY:
>
> Practice the way we make the Sign of the Cross.

The Greeting

The priest greets us all:

He says: *The Lord be with you.*

We respond: *And* _____ *your* _____ .

Usually on Sunday the priest says a few words of welcome.

4

The Penitential Act

For Teachers and Catechists

We have joined together with our brothers and sisters for this great prayer of worship—Eucharist, or Mass. To help us better prepare to receive all the gifts that come to us in Eucharist, we must first remember our failings. In the Penitential Act and the Lord, Have Mercy, we admit to ourselves, to God, and to our brothers and sisters gathered here that we have failed. We ask for prayers from Mary, the angels and saints, and from our community. Eucharist is a sacrament of forgiveness also, and in this part of Mass we ask for forgiveness and help to do better. So we pray to God, as Lord, as Christ, to have mercy on us. When we lay our failings down, we are able to participate fully by hearing the word and receiving the sacrament of Eucharist.

Second and third graders are able to know right from wrong. They just need help thinking through things and talking about them to become aware of how they fail to do the right thing. This is especially true in how they treat one another in relationships. Older children can come up with examples beyond their immediate experience, such as failing to pray for or to help God's children who live in poverty both here and in faraway places.

For Second and Third Graders

Talk with the children about times they may have done something wrong and then later apologized. Using their examples, draw out how different they felt afterward. Could they talk, play, be with the person in a better way then? Let them draw a "before and after" picture of forgiveness. Explain that the same thing is true with asking for forgiveness at the beginning of Mass. We can listen better to the scripture readings, sing and pray, and receive Holy Communion more reverently because we are more at peace. This is why we pray the Penitential Act and the Lord, Have Mercy.

For Fourth and Fifth Graders

In your own words, explain this part of Mass using "For Teachers and Catechists." Ask the children what new ideas they heard. Suggest that we can all take part in Mass more fully when we think in our hearts what failings to bring to the Lord. Together, brainstorm a "Review List" or "Examination of Conscience." If possible, write the list for all to see. Do a brief examination of conscience by having them close their eyes and think as you slowly and quietly review the list aloud. Invite them to talk about how doing this exercise before each Mass helps them participate better.

The Penitential Act

After the Greeting, the priest invites us to make the Penitential Act. This can take different forms.

- One is to pray the prayer called the Confiteor.

    I confess to almighty God,
    and to you, my brothers and sisters,
    that I have greatly sinned,
    in my thoughts and in my words,
    in what I have done, and what I have failed to do,

    And, striking the breast, they say:

    through my fault, through my fault,
    through my most grievous fault;
    therefore I ask blessed Mary, ever-Virgin,
    all the Angels and Saints,
    and you, my brothers and sisters,
    to pray for me to the Lord our God.

- The second option is a call and response between the priest and the assembly.

    The priest says: Have mercy on us, O Lord.

    We respond: *For we have sinned against you.*

    Then the priest says: Show us O Lord, your mercy.

    We respond: *And grant us your salvation.*

- Another way is to make petitions, usually led by the priest.

The Gloria

For Teachers and Catechists

The ancient and joyful prayer called the Gloria, or *Gloria in excelsis,* begins with the words that the angels sang at the birth of Jesus. As we consider this ancient prayer, read Luke 2:13–14. There, you will see that the first lines of this prayer are almost exactly as those that the angels sang. as they proclaimed the birth of Christ to the shepherds. We hear this verse from the Bible as the priest or deacon reads the Gospel during the Mass during the Night on the Nativity of the Lord.

As we sing the Gloria, we overflow with joy. Reflect on the words, "We praise you, / we bless you / we glorify you, / we give you thanks for your great glory . . . . What could be more joyous?

The basic forms of prayer are blessing, petition, intercession, thanksgiving, and praise (*Catechism of the Catholic Church* [CCC], 2644). We can see each of these expressions in the Gloria. In the first and second verse, of prayer as we bless, praise, and give thanksgiving. In the third verse, we petition the Lord to have mercy on us and to receive our prayer.

The final verse has us praising God again, as we call God, "The Holy One," "the Lord," the Most High and sing of "the glory of God the Father."

As we praise God with this prayer, we can see how the Gloria is a prayer of praise, as the CCC defines it "Prayer of praise is entirely disinterested and rises to God, lauds him, and gives him glory for his own sake, quite beyoned what he has done, but simply because HE IS" (2649)

Examining the prayer, we see that we name some of the many wonderful things God has done, such as taking away the sins of the world. We describe who God is: heavenly King, Most High, and almighty Father. We ask God to receive our prayer and to have mercy on us. We acknowledge that God is Father, Son, and Holy Spirit. In this hymn we give glory to God as we praise, bless, adore, and glorify God. We pray for peace to God's people of good will.

It is very appropriate to begin our celebration by praising God in this way and by reminding ourselves of who our wonderful God is.

Songs of praise are both common and important in both scripture and tradition. We see this in the many Psalms of praise; we see it in Mary's Magnificat (Luke 1:46–55) and in traditional prayers such as the Canticle of Saint Francis. The Gloria in Mass is above all in proclaiming our praise of God. It is interesting that, in the second century, the Church added a verse to the Our Father that expresses the praise of the Gloria: "For thine is the kingdom, the power, and the glory now and forever." In the last century the Church restored that doxology to the liturgy. We say, "For the kingdom, the power and the glory are yours

---

When the priest or minister sings or says, "Lord, have mercy," we respond with "Lord, have mercy." When the priest or minister sings or says, "Christ, have mercy," we respond with " _____ , _____ _____ ."

- On Sundays, especially during Easter Time, the priest may bless some water and sprinkle us, reminding us of our Baptism.

The Gloria

The Gloria is a song. As we sing it, our hearts are filled with praise for God. Sometimes the text is said rather than sung. We do not sing or recite the Gloria in Advent or Lent.

Glory to God in the highest,
    and on earth peace to people
        of good will.

We praise you,
we bless you,
we adore you,
we glorify you,
we give you thanks for your great glory,
Lord God, heavenly King,
O God, almighty Father.

/ now and for ever." These words continue to echo the words of praise in the Gloria.

For Second and Third Graders

Gloria

Talk with the children about the meaning and placement of the Gloria we sing at Mass. Brainstorm together some words we might use to describe someone we admire or love: great, wonderful, etc. Explain that the Gloria gives us words with which to praise God. Explain to the children that angels are beings who gloirfy God unceasingly(CCC, 350). We, too, should pray constantly throughout our days.

Put the following words from the Gloria on the board or chart for all to see. Under-line "Holy One; Lord; Most High." See how many ways the children can "define" those particular words. Let them suggest alternatives. Tell them that you are going to pray those words together like a cheer for God. Stand and say together enthusiastically.

You alone are the Holy One,
you alone are the Lord,
you alone are the Most High....

For Fourth and Fifth Graders

Gloria

Ask the students for examples of times they have been enthused at a game or a party, or times they have cheered for someone. Recall with them how we talk or even sing at such an occasion. Let them act out what they might say or sing duirng those times in a very quiet subdued manner, and then again but with enthusiasm. Draw a parallel with the Gloria at Mass. Provide the students with background on the prayer by reading Luke 2:11–14. This will help the students situate this hymn as the first sung praising God at the birth of Jesus. Point out to the students that this is a prayer to be prayed (preferably with voices raised in song) with enthusiasm and meaning. Let the students read over the words to the Gloria silently, then together either sing or recite the prayer with energy and meaning.

Have the children gather in groups to brainstorm words and phrases that they would use to describe Jesus Christ. Invite them to draw a picture depicting at least one of the words that they would use to describe our Savior.

Invite the children to find another place in the Mass that Jesus is called the Lamb of God. Ask them to turn to John 1:29 to read John the Baptist announcing " Behold, the Lamb of God . . . ."

Lord Jesus Christ, Only Begotten Son,
Lord God, Lamb of God, Son of the Father,
you take away the sins of the world,
    have mercy on us;
you take away the sins of the world,
    receive our prayer;
you are seated at the right hand of the Father,
    have mercy on us.

For you alone are the Holy One,
you alone are the Lord,
you alone are the Most High,
Jesus Christ,
with the Holy Spirit,
in the glory of God the Father.
Amen.

ACTIVITIES:

1. Read the Gloria and underline the lines that you find the most interesting.

2. Learn to sing the Gloria.

3. Find out why we don't pray the Gloria in Advent or Lent.

For Teachers and Catechists

After the Gloria the priest leads us in The Collect. This prayer begins with a few moments of quiet when the priest says, "Let us pray," so that we can gather our prayers and petitions. Appropriately, this prayer is also called The Collect, because in it we use both the time of silence and the words of the prayer to "collect" our thoughts in order to better participate in Mass. Before the priest prays aloud, we silently remember why we are here. We remember, too, that God is present here, and we think of the people and the intentions to be mindful of during this liturgy.

For Second and Third Graders

Collect

Talk with the group about how we all have people we care about. Share with the children who some of those people are to you—family or friends. Ask them to think of whom they care about that they'd like to ask God to bless. It may be someone with you that day or perhaps someone far away. Using colored markers and paper, let each child make a list. If they can't spell a name, they can draw a symbol or picture of the person. Take time to let them share their lists. Explain how this is the purpose of the Collect at Mass, and pray a Collect together. After you say, "Let us pray," invite them to bow their heads and think quietly about the names they wrote. After a bit of silence, continue with a brief prayer, asking God's blessing on all those we care for. Let the students pray "Amen" at the end of the prayer.

For Fourth and Fifth Graders

Collect

Engage the group in talking about collections of things—what they collect or what someone they know collects. Ask them about what someone means when they say, "I need to collect my thoughts."

Explain that before the priest starts the Collect, he says, "Let us pray." This provides the congregation with a chance to orient themselves to the sacred space and time.

They acknowledge that they are in God's presence and think to themselves of for whom they wish to pray during the liturgy.

For this exercise, you might want to borrow the chapel edition of *The Roman Missal* from the sacristy. If there is not a chapel edition, copy the Collects from last Sunday, the coming Sunday, and the next Sunday. With the children, pray two or three Collects (accent is on the first syllable.

from *The Roman Missal* with the students). Ask the students to whom the prayer is directed. (It usually is addressed to the Father, through Christ, in the Holy Spirit, *General Instruction of the Roman Missal*, 54.). Ask the students what it is that we are praying for in each of the prayers.

• Have your students do the activities on page 8 in the children's edition.

The Collect

The Collect is led by the priest.
He invites us to reflect for a short time when he says: *Let us pray.*

After our silent reflection, he then prays the prayer.

We respond by saying: A_____ .

② The Liturgy of the Word

For Teachers and Catechists

The Liturgy of the Word begins with the first scripture reading and ends with the Prayer of the Faithful. On Sundays and weekdays the First Reading is followed by the Responsorial Psalm. On Sundays and special days there is also a Second Reading.

Next is the Gospel Acclamation followed by the Gospel itself. After all of these scripture readings come the homily, the Creed, and the Prayer of the Faithful. This is a rich and important part of Mass. Christ comes to us in the consecrated bread and wine, and Christ also comes to us in the word.

We need to take these readings in just as we consume the bread and wine. When we eat food, it becomes part of us. When we are equally open to taking in the word of the Lord, it too can become part of us, part of who we are and how we live our life. Some scripture readings are easier to understand and apply to our life more readily than other readings. This is why we must listen carefully and take time to think about what they can mean to us. This is also why the homily is important. The homily helps us to understand the meaning of God's word we heard proclaimed so that we can live according to that word.

For Second and Third Graders

Display an outline of the Liturgy of the Word. Help the children understand the purpose of this part of the liturgy. Two ways we learn are by listening and by speaking. We sit and listen to the first readings, then stand for the very important Gospel. Next is an explanation from the priest in the homily. All of this is listening. We also speak. We speak in praying the Creed to show what we believe. In the Prayer of the Faithful we listen and respond in prayer for the world.

For Fourth and Fifth Graders

Give each child a list of the parts of the Liturgy of the Word in mixed-up order. Ask them to put them in sequence. As you review their answers, explain the purpose of each part. Question them about the posture for each and why we sit or stand for different parts. Brainstorm what they might do to pay close attention to the readings and the homily. Give each one four copies of an outline of the Liturgy of the Word on a sheet with spaces to write what they heard and learned from each of the readings and homily.

---

②

The Liturgy of the Word

At the end of the Collect we sit and prepare to hear the Word of the Lord.

On Sundays we listen to three readings and a psalm, all taken from the Bible. Christ himself is present and speaks to us in the readings, and the Holy Spirit moves in our hearts as we listen attentively. After the readings we listen to the homily, pray the Profession of Faith, and make our petitions in the Universal Prayer or Prayer of the Faithful. The readings are in a book called the _____.

9

The First Reading, Psalm, and Second Reading

For Teachers and Catechists

The scriptures are not just *read* at Mass. They are *proclaimed*! Good lectors practice them beforehand and proclaim them loudly and slowly enough to be heard and understood by everyone in church. The readings are that important. That is why our response to the readings is an important role for us to take. When we respond, "Thanks be to God" or sing the Responsorial Psalm with enthusiasm, we are making an act of faith. The book of Psalms is from the Old Testament. The Psalms are prayers of praise we sing or say at each Mass. Sometimes a lit candle is placed near the ambo (the place where the scriptures are proclaimed) as a sign that these words give light to our life. After each scripture we have a brief silence to think about what we just heard. At Sunday liturgy there are two readings before the Gospel and on weekdays, one reading followed by the Responsorial Psalm.

For Second and Third Graders

Help the children imagine someone standing in front of them and telling them something very important. Ask them how they would act while the person was talking and after he or she finished. Would they look somewhere else? Would they pay attention? Afterward, would they say something back or just sit there? Make the connection with the proclaiming of the scripture readings at Mass. Review what our responses are. Connect our response to the First Reading with "The word of the Lord," which the lector has said. Talk about the Psalm response and then choose a simple sung response to sing. After recalling how you began this conversation, encourage them to sing as though they had just been told something very important.

For Fourth and Fifth Graders

Using Bibles, look together at where these readings at Mass are located: the Old Testament or Acts of the Apostles for the First Reading, the book of Psalms, and for the Second Reading, the epistles or letters of Paul and other epistle writers, and the book of Revelation. Finally, let them look through the Psalms and find some verses they like. Let each child choose a verse and illustrate that line on colored paper, being sure to write the Psalm from which it came.

Invite the children to find the coming Sunday's readings in the Bible. Have them read the First Reading and the Psalm. Ask them what they have in common. Do they understand why that psalm was chosen? for that reading?

The First Reading

The First Reading is usually taken from the Old Testament (during Easter the First Reading is from the Acts of the Apostles, which is from the New Testament). We hear some of the great stories and sayings about God's love for the world and for us.

The reading finishes when the reader says: *The word of the Lord*.

We reply: _____ _____
_____ _____ .

The Responsorial Psalm

After the reading we have a short silence, and then we sing the psalm. The psalms are holy songs from the Bible. They can be sung in many different ways. Often we are invited to sing the response, although sometimes we say it together.

The Second Reading

Our next reading comes from the New Testament.

Again, the reading finishes when the reader says:

_____ _____ _____ _____ _____ .

And we reply: *Thanks be to God.*

The Gospel

For Teachers and Catechists

The Gospel, or Good News, is proclaimed at every Mass, whether on Sundays or weekdays. Parts of all accounts from the four evangelists—Matthew, Mark, Luke, and John—are used at different times over the three-year liturgical cycle. The Gospel tells the story of the life, death, and Resurrection of Jesus Christ. However, it is much more than a story. When the Gospel is proclaimed, it is Christ present to us now. We can take it in and let it change and challenge us. We have to listen with open ears, open hearts, and open minds for this gift to come into us, however. When we listen well, we understand the homily, which follows the Gospel in a way that helps us make good use of the lessons. It is even more helpful to read the Gospel before going to Mass. That way we have already let it "simmer" inside of us, to be even more able to take in the message it has for us today. This, too, helps us appreciate its richness when proclaimed at Mass.

For Second and Third Graders

As you talk with the children about the Gospel, help them realize that it is made up of stories about Jesus and his life and teachings. Mention what the Gospel from recent Sundays was, briefly retelling the stories. Ask them to name other stories they know from the Gospel. Choose a simple Gospel passage that can be acted out. Tell the story in your own words, and then help them act it out as you tell it again. Repeat this so that all the children have a chance to participate.

For Fourth and Fifth Graders

Invite the class to tell you some "Good News" that has happened to them or that they have read or heard. By using ideas from the "For Teachers and Catechists" on this page, explain how the Gospel is our shared Good News. Review where the Gospel comes in Mass, and talk together about those readings from recent Sundays. Because it is Good News, we are happy and sing Alleluia (except during Lent) before it is proclaimed. Teach them a common Alleluia used in the parish liturgy and sing it together. Hold the Book of the Gospels high and process to the front while the Alleluia is sung again. Then proclaim the Gospel for the coming Sunday. Together sing the Alleluia again. Tell them that *Alleluia* means "Praise God." We thank God for the Good News in Jesus.

The Gospel

It is now time for the Gospel. These special readings are taken from four writers, called evangelists. The names of the four evangelists are _____ , _____ , _____ , and _____ .

We know the Gospel is special because we often sing the word A _____ before it starts. And, we stand rather than sit. We also know it is special because we sometimes include the Gospel in a book called the _____ _____ _____ _____ . We process with this book and encircle it with candles. We incense it and we hold it high.

The person who reads the Gospel is either a deacon or a priest.

The Gospel begins with a dialogue:

Deacon or priest: *The Lord be with you.*

We respond: *And with your spirit.*

Deacon or priest: *A reading from the holy Gospel according to*

_____ .

We respond: _____ _____ _____

_____ , _____ .

After the reading is finished the priest says: *The Gospel of the Lord.*

11

The Homily

For Teachers and Catechists

The Church takes us through the Gospel over the course of the three-year Lectionary cycle. The scriptures and our tradition come to us as the source of our inspiration and guidance. The homily helps us understand and apply this wisdom to the way we live. It is food for the journey of the week ahead of us. Like the scriptures, the homily is to both comfort and challenge us. The homily is not just for inspiration while we are listening to it. It is our guide as we face the routine times of our life as well as the challenges we may face during the week. Sometimes the homily is about a special solemnity or feast we are celebrating. Many homilists say they read the scriptures for the next Sunday on the preceding Monday and throughout the week. That way they can pray with them and think about them both consciously and unconsciously throughout the week before they preach their homily. Christ is present at Mass in the scriptures proclaimed, and the homily helps us experience Christ's presence in those readings. To the extent we are aware that Christ is with us, we can live according to the Gospel with confidence and with insight.

For Second and Third Graders

Recall together times someone has read or told stories to the children. Perhaps it is parents or teachers, maybe babysitters or grandparents. Ask them to tell what they do after they hear a story. Do they ever talk about it some more or think about it? Perhaps they understand it better because of doing that. This is the kind of connection between the scriptures we hear at Mass and the homily. We listen to the Gospel. We know that in these stories or readings Christ is speaking to us. We can know and understand the message better if we have someone talk about it to us in the homily. Let the children recall anything they may remember from a homily they have heard.

For Fourth and Fifth Graders

If possible, invite a priest or deacon to be with the group. Ask him in advance to be prepared to explain how he prepares a homily and what he tries to accomplish in it. Then, if you have agreed in advance, let him do a scripture proclamation and brief (three minute) homily. Allow time for questions from the class.

Together with the children, read the scriptures for the coming Sunday, asking them to seek what themes might be in at least two of the readings. Explain that the First Reading and the Gospel are related. They should be able to see parallels in those readings.

We reply: _____ _____ _____ ,
_____ _____ _____ .

The Homily

In the homily the priest or deacon helps us understand the meanings of the Bible readings and the lessons they can teach us for our lives. We sit during the homily to help us listen more attentively.

The Profession of Faith

This prayer is also known as the Creed. It is sung or recited on Sundays and special days, and it involves all the people. We stand for the Profession of Faith. It is important to try to learn it.

I believe in one God,
    the Father almighty,
    maker of heaven and earth,
    of all things visible and invisible.

I believe in one Lord Jesus Christ,
    the Only Begotten Son of God,
    born of the Father before all ages.
    God from God, Light from Light,
    true God from true God,
    begotten, not made,
        consubstantial with the Father;
    through him all things were made.

The Profession of Faith

For Teachers and Catechists

Nicene Creed

The Nicene Creed is both a prayer and a statement of belief. It originated in 325 AD at the Council of Nicea. When we pray this creed, we echo what Catholics have prayed and believed through all those centuries.

What a wonderful reminder of what we hold as central to our faith! Praying it is a kind of catechetical lesson. The Creed begins with the Trinity, specifying the role of the Father as Creator. It reviews what we believe about Jesus Christ, his role in the Trinity, his life, death, and Resurrection as well as the future in his eternal kingdom. The Creed then states the important role of the Holy Spirit. Finally, we pray about our belief in the Catholic Church, the importance of Baptism, and our future bodily resurrection in eternity. This prayer is rich with meaning, history, and faith. It is to be prayed with conviction and one voice with the entire community. We can remember that people around the world are professing the same beliefs at Mass when they say the Creed.

The word *creed* comes from the Latin word *credo*, meaning "I believe." Belief in Jesus means accepting what God has revealed and living our life according to this belief. For Christians it means to trust in Jesus, to believe that he is the Christ and to accept what he teaches about our relationship with God and especially what that means in our daily life.

Recite the stanzas of the Creed together, reflecting on the words in each stanza. What does it mean that God created what is visible and invisible? What is invisble? Do the children think of angels as God's messengers who are invisible?

In the second stanza, the children may stumble over the word "consubstantial." This word tells about the divine nature of Jesus Christ. It explains that he is of the same substance of the Father. When children understand that, they can say the word more easily.

Another unusual word is "incarnate." Relate the word to Incarnation. The Word of God became flesh in the womb of the Virgin Mary.

In the last stanza of the Creed, the word "confess" might confuse the children. In this context, it means to acknowledge a belief.

Apostles' Creed

The shorter Apostles' Creed also states what we believe about the Father, the Son, and the Holy Spirit. The ending lines list other important beliefs: the Church, the communion of all believers—alive or dead—and the important belief that sins are forgiven and that we will rise again and live for eternity.

This Profession of Faith is called the Apostles' Creed, because it summarizes what the apostles handed down to us.

For us men and for our salvation
he came down from heaven,

[at this time , we bow]

and by the Holy Spirit was incarnate
of the Virgin Mary,
and became man.

[at this time we stand upright]

For our sake he was crucified under Pontius Pilate,
he suffered death and was buried,
and rose again on the third day
in accordance with the Scriptures.
He ascended into heaven
and is seated at the right hand of the Father.
He will come again in glory
to judge the living and the dead,
and his kingdom will have no end.

I believe in the Holy Spirit, the Lord, the giver of life,
who proceeds from the Father and the Son,
who with the Father and the Son is adored and glorified,
who has spoken through the Prophets.

I believe in one, holy, catholic and apostolic Church.
I confess one Baptsim for the forgiveness of sins
and I look forward to the resurrection of the dead
and the life of the world to come. Amen.

During the Easter Vigil, catechumens are asked three questions prior to their Baptism. These three questions summarize the three parts of this creed: "Do you believe in God, the almighty Father, creator of heaven and earth? Do you believe in Jesus Christ, his only Son, our Lord, who was born of the Virgin Mary . . . ? Do you believe in the Holy Spirit and in his work?" This same summary is asked of the community at the Easter Vigil. It has been a custom since the third century, and we carry on this tradition today.

For Second and Third Graders

Prepare for each child a large paper with the words to the Nicene Creed on the bottom half. On the top half have a line for them to put the words "I BELIEVE" in large colored letters. Read through the Creed slowly together. Have them find the first time those two words appear and underline them. Talk with the children about what that part of the Creed says. Then go to the next "I Believe" and explain it until you have covered the entire Creed. Let them decorate their "belief banner."

If possible, obtain *The Roman Missal* from the church (it will probably be in the sacristy). Reverently open it to the Creed and show the children the words of the Nicene Creed that the priest leads the community in praying. Point out the words that match the banner they made. Talk about when it is that we pray the Creed at Mass, reviewing all that comes before it. Explain that the word *Creed* means "I believe." Stress how their saying this prayer at Mass shows that they believe all that is in this prayer. Encourage them to say it strongly at Mass to show that they mean what they say.

For Fourth and Fifth Graders

Depending upon how many are in the group, divide a copy of the Creed into sections and give them out to small groups. Let each group work together to write an explanation of how they understand their part of the Creed. Have each group share what they wrote by reading that part of the Creed and explaining it to the large group.

You will need to elaborate and clarify each piece as it is presented. When all are finished, stand and proclaim the Creed together.

If possible, visit the baptismal font in church together. In advance, obtain the *Rite of Christian Initiation of Adults* and turn to the Rite of Baptism for the Easter Vigil. Reverently show the students the three questions from the Easter Vigil and/or Baptismal Rite. After explaining these questions (see For Teachers and Catechists), reenact the asking of the questions with the students responding. At the end have each student bless himself or herself with holy water, reciting the words to the Sign of the Cross aloud. Remind the children that this is an expression of belief in the Father, Son, and Holy Spirit.

We may also say a shorter form of the Creed. This creed is called the Apostles' Creed. We also say this prayer when we pray the Rosary.

I believe in God,
the Father almighty,
Creator of heaven and earth,
and in Jesus Christ, his only Son, our Lord,

[Bow until after the words "Virgin Mary."]

who was conceived by the Holy Spirit,
born of the Virgin Mary,
suffered under Pontius Pilate,
was crucified, died and was buried;
he descended into hell;
on the third day he rose again from the dead;
he ascended into heaven,
and is seated at the right
    hand of God the Father almighty;
from there he will come to judge the living and the dead.

I believe in the Holy Spirit,
the holy catholic Church,
the communion of saints,
the forgiveness of sins,
the resurrection of the body,
and life everlasting. Amen.

Prayer of the Faithful

For Teachers and Catechists

At this point during Mass, the Prayer of the Faithful (also called the Universal Prayer) is prayed by the baptized members of the assembly. You may point out to the children the universal nature of these prayers, as prayers are offered for the salvation of all. The celebrant invites us to pray these prayers and we stand to do so. One person speaks the prayers in the name of the assembly. The community adds its voice to each intercession, either in spoken or sung response. This response makes these petitions to God in our name. Together we bring the needs of the human family to God—for the needs of the Church, the world, the oppressed, and the local community. In a real sense, these petitions are our response to the presence of God that has come to us in the Liturgy of the Word. This last action of the first part of Mass calls out to God the needs of the world in which we live and asks for God's help and blessing. It is the whole world that is prayed for here, not just us and our personal needs. We bring the entire world with us to the liturgy and place it before God in this prayer.

For Second and Third Graders

Bring with you whatever was prayed in the Universal Prayer in church last Sunday. Help the children recall this part of Mass, noting that it comes after the Creed. If there was no Creed, the intercessions follow the homily. Remind the children of the significance of standing for these prayers as a sign of their importance. Also explain that these are not prayers of the person who reads them, but they are the prayers of all of those gathered. Ask them how we can make them our prayer, then say or sing together a usual response in your parish. Then invite them to stand and prayerfully use that response as you pray the prayers from Sunday's liturgy.

For Fourth and Fifth Graders

Review this part of Mass with the group. Remind them of its placement in the Liturgy of the Word. Point out that this is the last part of the Liturgy of the Word before we transition to the Liturgy of the Eucharist. Assign small groups to each of the four areas of the petitions: The Church, the world, the needs of those who are burdened in some way, the needs of our community and family. Let each group write three petitions for their assigned area.

- Have your students do the activity on page 16 in the children's edition.

Prayer of the Faithful

In the readings we have heard what God has done for us. As we remain standing we now ask God to look after everyone and everything in creation.

We usually ask God to watch over four areas.

- We ask God to help the Church be strong and faithful.

- We ask God to encourage and advise our local, national, and world leaders.

- We ask God to look after anyone who is in need, such as the hungry, the sick, the cold, and those without homes.

- We ask God for the things we need in our own community and family.

These prayers are truly our prayers—the Church, those who have been baptized—and each one is led by a person from the congregation or the deacon.

For Teachers and Catechists

The Liturgy of the Word consists of a sequence of actions or parts. The Liturgy of the Word and what follows in the Liturgy of the Eucharist are both equally necessary to have Eucharist. Christ is present in both parts of the Mass. In fact, Christ is present in the word, most especially in the consecrated bread and wine, in the priest, and the community assembled (*Constitution on the Sacred Liturgy*, 7). The more deeply we understand and believe that, the more deeply we can benefit from Christ's presence to us. It is helpful for children to learn about and understand the parts and the purpose of each part of the Mass. That will help them grow in their openness to receive all that is offered and grow in deepening their participation in this source and summit of our faith

You could help the children to become more immersed in the Liturgy of the Word through the Psalms and readings. Begin a session slowly reciting the psalm for the coming week. Ask the children about the point the psalmist is making. Is the Psalmist thanking God? Why would he be thankful? Is the psalmist asking for something from God? Is the Psalm a prayer of petition? What emotion is the psalmist portraying? Is he upset? Is he joyful? Is he trusting in the Lord? Are there words praising God in the Psalm? Do the children notice that the psalmist changes emotions during the Psalm? Ask the children to copy the coming Sunday's psalm. One verse of the Psalm will be enough for the younger children to copy. The older children might want to read Sunday's Psalm in the context of the whole Psalm. from the Bible.

For Second and Third Graders

Make a large cardboard wheel or circle with the words "Liturgy of the Word" in the center. Put the name of each part of the Liturgy of the Word in a different color around the center: First Reading, Responsorial Psalm, Second Reading, Gospel Acclamation, Gospel, Homily, Profession of Faith, Prayer of the Faithful. Turn the wheel and review each part, letting them first tell you all they recall about each one.

For Fourth and Fifth Graders

Prepare a page for each student containing a list of the eight parts of the Liturgy of the Word (see the above list under "For Second and Third Graders"). Do not put the parts in order, but have them mixed up. Let the students cut out the names of the parts and arrange them in the correct order. Alternatively, they could number them sequentially. As you review the parts of the Liturgy of the Word with them, let the students make any corrections on their sequence.

ACTIVITY:

Write a prayer for each of these four areas.

1. _____
   _____
   _____
   _____
   _____

2. _____
   _____
   _____
   _____
   _____

3. _____
   _____
   _____
   _____
   _____

4. _____
   _____
   _____
   _____
   _____

③ The Liturgy of the Eucharist

For Teachers and Catechists

Now begins the Liturgy of the Eucharist. We use the word *Eucharist* to describe our most important prayer as Catholics — Mass. The word is also used to describe the sacrament that is consecrated and received during Mass: the Body and Blood of Christ in Holy Communion. The word *Eucharist* comes from the Greek word *eucharistein*, which means "thanksgiving." (To this day, if you want to say "thank you" in Greek you say *efharistó*!) Mass is a great prayer of thanksgiving, which the Church offers to God the Father. We give thanks to God for all the blessings of our lives, but above all we thank God for the gift of his Son, Jesus Christ. Our principal way of worshipping Christ present in Eucharist is to gather with other believers, the Body of Christ, to celebrate Mass and to receive the sacrament of his Body and Blood in Holy Communion.

For Second and Third Graders

Before this lesson, ask your students to bring in photographs of people they love and for whom they are grateful. During class, ask your students to share thoughts about people in the photographs. Why do they love them? What do you and your loved ones do together? Why are these things so special? Remind them that we get together at Mass because we are one family in Christ. We come together to give God thanks and praise for Christ Jesus, so grateful are we for his love. Have them make a class collage with the various photographs. Hang the collage in the classroom with the title "We give thanks for God's family."

For Fourth and Fifth Graders

Remind your students that *Eucharist* means "thanksgiving." Ask them, as Christians, for what are we grateful? What do we come together for? Why is this important? How is Holy Communion important to your life of faith?

Have the students make thank-you cards to God. In the cards they can list the things that they are most thankful for. They could also make a collage using cut outs from magazines and photographs that they bring from home to school. The pictures represent the people or things for which they are most thankful. Have the students present their collages to the rest of the class.

③

The Liturgy of the Eucharist

This part of Mass has three stages. The first is when we prepare the gifts of bread and wine. The second is when the great prayer of thanksgiving is prayed. The third stage is when we receive Holy Communion.

Presentation and Preparation of the Gifts

We bring forward to the priest the bread and wine that will be consecrated in the great prayer of thanksgiving. We may also bring some water. During the procession the people sit.

17

Presentation and Preparation of the Gifts

For Teachers and Catechists

The altar is prepared with the altar cloth and *The Roman Missal* with prayers for the priest. Wine and water are poured into the chalice, and bread in the form of hosts is brought to the table. In preparation for Eucharist, the priest symbolically washes his hands, saying a prayer, asking that he be cleansed from his sins and worthy to lead the community in this great sacrificial prayer. Our gifts are brought forth to be offered as well. In the early Church, people brought food from their homes and their fields to be shared with those who were in need. We still remember this custom on Holy Thursday when food for the hungry is brought forward. Our monetary gifts to be used for the community and the needy are also brought forward at this time. Eucharist is about sharing spiritual food for our spiritual hungers and needs and sharing physical food for those who do not have enough to eat.

For Second and Third Graders

Bring a wrapped gift to show the children.

- Talk with the children about the necessary steps in getting a gift ready to offer to a person and how it is important to take care in that preparation.
- Explain how we take care in Mass to prepare the gifts we are going to offer to God in the next part of the liturgy called the Liturgy of the Eucharist.
- Unwrap the gift and explain its purpose.
- On a page divided into sections, invite the children to draw a colored picture of each of the items used in the Presentation and Preparation of the Gifts.
- On separate pages, have a picture of the water, wine, chalice, paten for the bread, hosts, food to be offered, collection baskets for money. Put these in the gift box.

For Fourth and Fifth Graders

Explain or review for the students this part of Mass. Especially help them see the importance of food both for the body and the spirit. Let them tell what they know about the Presentation and Preparation of the Gifts and how the actions of this part of the liturgy are carried out in their parish church. If possible, give them a tour of the sacristy and especially look at the liturgical vessels and vestments. If that is not possible, do a role-play of this part of Mass with them.

- Have your students do the activity on page 18 in the children's edition.

As the gifts are brought forward we may sing.

The bread will become our food and the wine will become our drink. They are the food and drink of heaven blessed by God and shared by him with us.

ACTIVITY:

What are some of the different meanings we give to the words *bread* and *wine*? For instance, bread can signify food. What are some others?

Bread can signify	Wine can signify
_____	_____
_____	_____
_____	_____

Because all good things come from God, we too are encouraged to be generous. Sometimes during the Presentation and Preparation of the Gifts, money and gifts are collected for the poor and the needs of the Church.

Holding the bread, the priest prays:
Blessed are you, Lord God of all creation,
for through your goodness we have received
the bread we offer you:
fruit of the earth and work of human hands,
it will become for us the bread of life.

We respond: _____ _____ _____
_____ _____ .

18

For Teachers and Catechists

We continue to prepare the gifts to be offered. Before the consecration, the priest and the community ask God to bless the bread and wine. The beautiful prayers over the bread and the wine at this point give credit to God that we even have these gifts. We bless God, reminding ourselves that it is because God has made all of creation that we have these gifts to offer. God's creation has provided the bread and wine, which come from the earth. We remind ourselves that humans have grown the wheat and grapes we now prepare to offer. We listen to the words the priest prays, which acknowledge that, in this Eucharist, they will become not just physical food but the bread of life and our spiritual drink. Then the priest invites us to pray together that this, our sacrifice, will be acceptable to God the Father.

Here are the two prayers the priest prays:

Blessed are you, Lord, God of all creation,
for through your goodness we have recived
this bread we offer you:
fruit of the earth and work of human hands,
it will become for us the bread of life.

Blessed are you, Lord, God of all creation.
for through your goodness we have received
the wine we offer you:
fruit of the vine and work of human hands,
it will become our spiritual drink.

For Second and Third Graders

Display the two prayers over the bread and the wine, which the priest prays as he holds up each. Underline each phrase as you call to the children's attention that we have this food because God created nature, farms, and vineyards produced with the help of human hands. We will therefore be fed by eating and drinking what God has created. Remind them that it will be spiritual food when it becomes the Body and Blood of Christ later in the liturgy. Invite the children to stand and raise their hands as if they are holding the bread or wine as all pray together the prayer of the priest and our response to it.

For Fourth and Fifth Graders

Review this part of the Presentation and Preparation of the Gifts with the students. Emphasize that we are still preparing the gifts for the great offering to God, which will only come later after the bread and wine have been consecrated. As they look at the two prayers of the priest as he holds the bread and wine, challenge them to draw a colored picture of the stages each prayer describes of the bread and the wine.

Holding the cup of wine, the priest prays a similar prayer:
Blessed are you, Lord God of all creation,
for through your goodness we have received
the wine we offer you:
fruit of the vine and work of human hands,
it will become our spiritual drink.

We respond: _____ _____ _____
_____ _____ .

The priest leads us as we ask God to accept our gifts:

Priest: *Pray, brothers and sisters,*
that my sacrifice and yours
may be acceptable to God,
the almighty Father.

We respond: *May the Lord accept the sacrifice*
at your hands
for the praise and glory of his name,
for our good
and the good of all his holy Church.

At this stage we stand up and the priest prays the Prayer over the Gifts.

We respond by praying: *A_____.*

The Eucharistic Prayer

For Teachers and Catechists

Although the entire Mass is a prayer of thanksgiving, the Eucharistic Prayer holds a special place. It is the great prayer of thanksgiving that the priest prays in our name. It is important that we pray this prayer by listening carefully to what he prays and by making it our prayer in the silence of our hearts. In addition to Mass we pray at other times, of course. We pray to ask for forgiveness. Some of our prayers are prayers of petition, or asking God for help. Some prayers are prayers of praise in which we give praise and glory to God. Others are prayers of adoration. In these prayers our words show that we adore the God who created us, redeemed us, and loves us forever. Prayers of thanksgiving—even apart from the great prayer of thanksgiving in Mass—help us remember the many reasons we have to be thankful.

For Second and Third Graders

Talk with the children about the great prayer of thanksgiving, the Eucharistic Prayer, explaining what it is and how they can join in even though the priest is praying it aloud in our name. Give examples of other times people might speak for an entire group. Ask them for examples. Remind them that this is the most important "Thank you" prayer the Church has, and that it is important for them to listen and agree with it in their minds and hearts. Give each child a page with the words THANK YOU printed in large open letters for them to color.

For Fourth and Fifth Graders

As you explain the Eucharistic Prayer, review the different kinds of prayers and write the name of each for all to see. Talk together about some of the things we might say in each of the types of prayers. Encourage the children to think about why we need all different kinds of prayer. Let each student compose a brief prayer (even if just a sentence or two) of each of the kinds of prayers. Only share them if the children are comfortable doing so. Close by reminding them where in Mass the Eucharistic Prayer comes and why it is so important to listen carefully and make it our own prayer.

For Teachers and Catechists

The presence of Christ in Eucharist is an essential belief for Catholics. Some Christian denominations believe that their Communion is a remembrance. For Catholics, although we pray in the Eucharistic Prayer that Christ said to "do this in remembrance of me," we hold that it is more than a mere memorial. We believe that Christ is truly present in both the consecrated bread and wine. This is one of the most important mysteries of our faith. The bread and the wine obviously do not change in their appearance, but rather in their substance. Christ is now fully and totally present in

The Eucharistic Prayer

The word *Eucharist* means "thanksgiving." It comes from the Greek language.

This is the great prayer in Mass. During this prayer we give thanks to God for creating the world, for making us, and for watching over us. Especially we praise and thank God for sending us Christ who showed us how to live. We do not forget God's other gift, the gift of the Holy Spirit who continually is with us and opens our eyes to grace and peace.

both of these species. We are encouraged to do as Christ told his followers at the Last Supper: "Take and eat." "Take and drink." In the last century the tradition and privilege of both eating and drinking was returned to common practice. Christ is equally present in both species, and we receive the fullness of his presence even when we only receive the consecrated bread.

In many places we are blessed to be able to receive both the Body of Christ and the Blood of Christ. It is in the Eucharistic Prayer that this miracle of change from bread and wine to Christ's Body and Blood takes place.

For Second and Third Graders

Let the children tell ways that they remember people who are far away or perhaps have died. Lead them to recall ways we are reminded of Christ, especially in our church, such as the crucifix, pictures in the windows, Stations of the Cross. Stress that the most special way is at Mass in the consecrated bread and wine. However, this is more than just remembering our Lord because the bread and wine are now changed into Christ's Body and Blood so that he can come to us again. We cannot understand fully how this happens, but we believe it because Jesus told us that at the Last Supper. Have the children draw a picture of one way Christ is remembered today.

For Fourth and Fifth Graders

Read aloud for the class Matthew 26:26–28, which is one account of the Last Supper. Jesus was celebrating the Jewish Passover meal when he gave us this sacrament. Discuss the connection between the words in Matthew and the words of the consecration at Mass. Write them together on a board or chart for all to see. Explain what we mean by "words of institution" when the bread and wine are changed into Christ's Body and Blood. Let the students fold a paper in half. On one half have them draw a picture of the Last Supper, and on the other half, a picture of Eucharist today.

• Have your students do the activity on page 21 in the children's edition.

ACTIVITY:

Complete this sentence:

Some of the things I am thankful for are

_____

_____

_____

_____

In the Eucharistic Prayer we call upon God the Father through the Holy Spirit to bless the bread and wine to become the Body and Blood of Christ. When we eat and drink the consecrated bread and wine at Holy Communion we are united with Christ, the Son of God and our brother.

The prayer has many parts.

The Preface Dialogue

Still standing, we begin together like this:

Priest: *The Lord be with you.*

We respond: *And with your spirit.*

Priest: *Lift up your hearts.*

We respond: *We lift them up to the Lord.*

Priest: *Let us give thanks to the Lord our God.*

We respond: *It is right and just.*

The Holy, Holy, Holy (the Sanctus)

For Teachers and Catechists

The Holy, Holy, Holy is a prayer that actually continues the Preface that the priest prays. This part of the prayer is called the Preface Acclamation. It is at this point that the people and the choir join in and sing this ancient prayer/song. The Holy, Holy, Holy is part of the liturgy in both the Eastern and Western Church. It is an ancient prayer that has been prayed at Mass since before the year 400. It is clearly in two parts. Scripture inspires both parts, and each part ends with "Hosanna in the highest." The first section comes from Isaiah 6:33. The second part, from Matthew 21, hearkens to Jesus' arrival, on a donkey, with his disciples into Jerusalem. The people shouted out their praise and hope for salvation with these words. After the Hosanna, the priest prays over the bread and wine and Christ becomes present in both these elements just as he promised at the Last Supper.

For Second and Third Graders

Help the children see where this prayer comes in Mass and why it is important to pray and sing it with enthusiasm. Read or tell the story of the people shouting and praising Jesus as he rode into Jerusalem on a donkey (Matthew 21, especially verse 9). Practice the words with them, encouraging them to sing them with energy. Have a little parade around the room singing this prayer; if possible, use pom-poms or something to imitate the palms that the people waved when Jesus came.

For Fourth and Fifth Graders

Review the story and roots of this part of the Preface. Read or tell the story from Matthew 21:1–11, Mark 11:1–10 or Luke 19:28–40 about Jesus entering the Holy City. These accounts from the Gospel are read during Year A, B, and C, respectively. (John 12:12–16 also may be read during Year B.) Invite the students to compare and contrast these readings. What elements are in each reading?

Help them make connections with times they are enthused as a group at celebrations and how they participate. Learn one or two of the usual melodies for the Holy, Holy, Holy from your parish, or school hymnal. When the students are comfortable singing themse melodies, remind them of the enthusiasm of the people on the road to Jerusalem.

Ask the children to recall the procession in their parish on Palm Sunday of the Lord's Passion. Help them visualize the day and how they feel as they receive their palms and process with them? Do they notice a certain joyfulness that day?

Then the priest continues the prayer by praising the things that God has done for us and for creation.

The Holy, Holy, Holy (the Sanctus)

All together we respond with a song of praise:

> Holy, Holy, Holy Lord God of hosts.
> Heaven and earth are full of your glory.
> Hosanna in the highest.
> Blessed is he who comes in the name of the Lord.
> Hosanna in the highest.

In this acclamation we are united with the angels and all creation.

ACTIVITY:

Learn to sing the Holy, Holy, Holy. Use the musical setting your parish church uses.

After this acclamation we kneel. The priest then continues the Eucharistic Prayer. During this part of the prayer he invites the Holy Spirit to bless the bread and the wine, which become the Body and Blood of Christ. He does this because this is what Jesus asked us to do to remember him. He becomes present to us, and in Holy Communion is united with us. Jesus also invites the Holy Spirit to bless us, so that we will become more like him.

Memorial Acclamation

For Teachers and Catechists

Now we have our second of the three important acclamations sung during the Eucharistic Prayer. After the words of consecration, we affirm our faith in this mystery by joining in one of the three options for this acclamation. It is important for all of the assembly to sing. The Eucharistic acclamations are our way of affirming what has just taken place on the altar. It is no longer bread and wine, but now Christ is present in both these elements. It is a great mystery of our faith in which we prayerfully acclaim our belief.

For Second and Third Graders

The duration of the Eucharistic Prayer can be a long time for young children to pay attention to what is happening. Tell them they have three times to join in this important prayer. Let them know that the priest says or sings four words to let us know it is our turn to join him in this prayer. The words are "The mystery of faith." Write these words for all to see and practice them together. Then, review with them the options for our response. Practice together the one your parish most often uses.

For Fourth and Fifth Graders

Help the students see that the three times we join the priest—the Holy, Holy, Holy, the Memorial Acclamation, and the Great Amen—are important. In each one, the members of the assembly join together to proclaim their belief in what is happening on the altar—the miracle of the Eucharistic presence of Christ. After reviewing the three options, look at the words of invitation of the priest. Put the following words up for the students to see:

• Mystery
• Faith

In small groups have them come up with as many explanations/descriptions of those words as they can. Share these with the entire group. Then pray the options we use as our response.

The options are:

*We proclaim your Death, O Lord,
and profess your Resurrection
until you come in glory.*

*When we eat this Bread and drink
    this Cup,
we proclaim your Death, O Lord,
until you come again.*

*Save us, Savior of the world,
for by your Cross and Resurrection,
you have set us free.*

As the prayer continues, we hear the priest recall the words and actions of Jesus at the Last Supper when he gave us Eucharist and asked us to continue it as a memorial of him.

Memorial Acclamation

During the Eucharistic Prayer we praise God out loud and all together with an acclamation.

The priest leads us: *The mystery of faith.*

We have three ways of praising God:

*We proclaim your _____ , O Lord,
and profess your _____
until you come _____ .*

or

*When we eat this _____ and _____
    this Cup,
we _____ your Death, O Lord,
until you come again.*

or

*Save us, Savior of the _____ ,
for by your Cross and _____ ,
you have set us free.*

The priest then continues with the prayer, asking God to grant our requests.

The Doxology (Amen)

For Teachers and Catechists

The great prayer that the priest has been praying in the name of the assembly comes to a dramatic conclusion with the words of praise in the Doxology. We are praising God the Father through the Holy Spirit by offering him the great gift of his Son who sacrificed his life for us and is now present in the consecrated bread and wine. The priest and deacon hold these Eucharistic elements up high while they are offered to the Father with all honor and glory. Again, very significantly, the assembly makes the prayer their own with their Great Amen. The word *Amen* is one of a few Hebrew words used in the liturgy. The word means that you agree with what has just been said. This is why it is said or sung enthusiastically as we hear the closing words of the Eucharistic Prayer. Amen is used in the Old and New Testaments as a word of affirmation or confirmation of what was just said. We continue to use it with that meaning in our Eucharist today.

For Second and Third Graders

Explain to the children the purpose and importance of this closing of the great prayer. Elicit examples of how they say "Yes!" to something they are enthused or excited about. This is what we do in the Great Amen at Mass. Let them give examples of other times they use this word, and make the connection with its meaning there also. Give each one a paper with large open letters of AMEN! for them to color and decorate.

- Have all students do the activity on page 27 in the children's editon.

For Fourth and Fifth Graders

Allow time for the students to carefully read the words of the Doxology and discover to whom the prayer is giving honor and glory. Explain how it is praising God the Father. Then have them tell where all three persons of the Trinity are named. Remind them that this great prayer concludes with this important and wonderful line of praise. Discuss the meaning of the word *Amen* (literally, "so be it") as our way of agreeing with what the priest has been praying. This is how we make this offering of the consecrated bread and wine our offering to God the Father also.

The Doxology (Amen)

The Eucharistic Prayer ends with a great act of praise. The priest and deacon hold high the consecrated bread and wine, and give glory to God:

> Through him, and with him, and in him,
> O God almighty Father,
> in the unity of the Holy Spirit,
> all glory and honor is yours,
> for ever and ever.

We bring the prayer to an end when we sing:
A_____ .

We now stand.

The Lord's Prayer

For Teachers and Catechists

This prayer is called the Lord's Prayer because it is what Jesus taught when he was asked how to pray. It is a common prayer in the sense that it is universally known and prayed among all Christians. However, it is both a simple and a very challenging prayer. In it we acknowledge that we are citizens of both heaven and earth. We humbly ask for what we need. Our daily bread can be food, spiritual strength, moral courage, or any number of other needs of which we might not even be aware. The very serious challenge to the one who prays it is in the asking for forgiveness. Here we say that God should not forgive us any greater than we are forgiving others. Finally, we acknowledge that evil and temptation are stronger than we are, and it is God's help that will lead us away from it. The Lord's Prayer is in the Gospel according to Luke 11:2–4 as well as Matthew 6:9–13. At Mass it is appropriate that the priest and people pray this aloud together, as we are one community trying to live out this prayer that Jesus gave us.

For Second and Third Graders

Make sure all the children can see the words of the Our Father. Review where it comes in Mass. Stress that everyone in the assembly prays it together. This familiar prayer contains some difficult concepts. Explain the words in a way that the children can grasp the meaning behind them. Go through the prayer slowly, asking the students to help you make up gestures for each part. Standing in a circle, pray it together with the gestures that just were created.

For Fourth and Fifth Graders

Read from the scriptures the story of Jesus giving this prayer to his disciples. Spend time going through the Our Father line by line, getting the students' ideas about the meaning and adding your own. Allow time for the students to quietly choose what they think is a most important phrase or thought in the prayer and why it is significant. Ask them to write their thoughts about their choice. Invite the students to share what they wrote. Then stand and pray it together.

The Lord's Prayer

As the time for Holy Communion comes closer we make special preparation. We pray the prayer that Jesus himself taught us. This prayer, the Our Father, reminds us that God gives us our bread each day.

Priest and people all pray together:

> Our Father, who art in heaven,
> hallowed be thy name;
> thy kingdom come;
> thy will be done on earth as it is in heaven.
> Give us this day our daily bread;
> and forgive us our trespasses
> as we forgive those who trespass against us;
> and lead us not into temptation,
> but deliver us from evil.

After the Lord's Prayer, the priest prays:

Deliver us, Lord, we pray, from every evil,
graciously grant peace in our days,
that, by the help of your mercy,
we may be always free from sin
and safe from all distress,
as we await the blessed hope
and the coming of our Savior, Jesus Christ.

We respond: *For the kingdom,*
the _____ and _____
_____ are yours,
_____ and _____ _____ .

Sign of Peace

For Teachers and Catechists

At the Last Supper, the night before Jesus died, the very night when Jesus gave the apostles the bread and wine that were his Body and Blood, he said, "I leave you peace; my peace I give you" (John 14:27). The first thing Jesus said to his friends when he appeared to them after his Resurrection was, "Peace be with you." The Sign of Peace at Mass continues the tradition and the ritual given to us by Christ. The priest greets us with the words of Christ offering us peace. Before we receive the sacred bread and wine, we do as the priest (or deacon) directs us: "Let us offer each other the sign of peace." This ritual of turning to those near us signifies that we are one with each other; we are here together, not alone. In the Our Father we prayed that God would forgive us as we forgive others. Here we offer a sign of that reconciliation to one another. It is also a sign of how we intend to be with others in our life—a person offering peace and reconciliation.

For Second and Third Graders

Explore with the children examples they can think of about what *peace* means. It has many meanings and layers for all of us. The examples of children this age will mostly be personal and individual, although there will be some awareness of large conflicts. Remind the students of how important it is to Christ that we be are persons of peace. Use Jesus' examples. Let the students give examples of how they might help bring peace in their family or at school. Talk about the Sign of Peace at Mass, reviewing where it comes. Remind the students that the Sign of Peace is a holy ritual. Show how it is done, then let them offer peace to one another.

For Fourth and Fifth Graders

Help the children imagine how the apostles must have felt after Jesus died. Peter had denied him; most of them had deserted him. The Gospel only tells of John being at the cross. Did they feel they had abandoned him? Would they have felt disturbed.

Would they have desired to be forgiven? Christ did not ask them to apologize. he just offered peace. How would that make them feel? Have they ever been forgiven before they apologized? Is this the way Christians should act?

Encourage the children to brainstorm and list ways peace is needed in our homes and at school. Let each group share their list. Discuss where and how they can have an effect on the examples they gave. Talk with them about the importance of peace in the message of Christ to all of us who are followers of Christ. Review the Sign of Peace at Mass, explaining its importance as a ritual. Make the connection between sharing this ritual and what we prayed in the Our Father, and receiving the Body and Blood of Christ in Holy Communion.

Sign of Peace

Part of our preparation for Holy Communion is to receive the gift of peace that Christ gives us.

The priest says:
Lord Jesus Christ,
who said to your Apostles:
Peace, I leave you, my peace I give you;
look not on our sins,
but on the faith of your Church,
and graciously grant her peace and unity
in accordance with your will.

Who live and reign for ever and ever.

We respond: _____ .

The priest says: *The peace of the Lord be with you always.*

We reply: _____ _____
_____ _____ .

The deacon or priest says: *Let us offer each other the sign of peace.*

We now receive this gift from our neighbor and offer this same peace to all around us. We do this by shaking _____ and saying, "Peace be _____ _____"
to those who are near us.

26

Lamb of God (Fraction of the Bread)

For Teachers and Catechists

Two things happen simultaneously as we come closer to the time of sharing the sacred meal in Holy Communion. The priest is preparing the consecrated bread and wine for the community to receive them. He is at the altar, breaking the bread and saying the words of the Fraction of the Bread. If there is more than one Communion minister, the priest places the hosts within the vessels. He pours the consecrated wine into the vessels for the Communion ministers to serve. While the priest is doing this, the assembly is praying the Lamb of God together. In this way, we too are preparing to come to the table.

In this prayer we ask God to take away our sins and to grant us peace. We address Christ in this three-part prayer as the Lamb of God. This title of reverence is filled with meaning. In the Old Testament the Passover lamb was sacrificed as an offering to God. On the cross, Jesus was sacrificed for all of us. He became the Lamb of God who had been prophesied. John the Baptist announced to the crowd: "Behold, the Lamb of God, who takes away the sin of the world" (John 1:29).

For Second and Third Graders

Provide large outlines of an image of a lamb for each child. In large letters at the top of the page, have the word MERCY. At the bottom of the page, have the word PEACE. Spend time talking about these two words with the children, giving many examples and eliciting examples from them. Then explain that in the Lamb of God prayer this is what we are asking Christ to give us—mercy and peace. Talk to them about the lamb being the symbol of Christ whom we are addressing in this prayer. Let them decorate their lamb, and have each one give and receive another's picture as a gesture of peace to each other.

For Fourth and Fifth Graders

Help the students think of people or examples of mercy:

- times someone has shown leniency to someone who has done something wrong;
- acts of compassion;
- help given to others in need.

List some of the suggestions. Do the same with examples of peace, helping them think about internal peace, peace between two people or within a family, as well as world peace. After the discussion use the Lamb of God as an example of a prayer for mercy and peace. Allow time for the children to review the examples on the board. Then let each one choose either word to write his or her prayer about mercy or peace.

ACTIVITY:

Do you know of other forms of greeting that people use across the world? (For instance, in Korea people bow to one another.)

_____

_____

_____

_____

Lamb of God (Fraction of the Bread)

The priest breaks the consecrated bread and pours the consecrated wine so that we can receive Holy Communion. It is a sign that we all eat the same food together and are like one family united together. Jesus broke the bread at the Last Supper.

27

Communion

For Teachers and Catechists

As the priest holds up the sacred species before us, he reminds us that this is the Lamb of God who takes away all sin. Then he says: "Blessed are those called to the supper of the Lamb." We can only imagine how the apostles felt at the Last Supper. Celebrating the Passover meal with Jesus, the apostles were given the incredible gift of his presence now in the bread and wine he blessed and shared with them. We have the same gift of Christ's presence in Holy Communion. Our experience of coming to the supper table of the altar is just as real as the apostles' experience was with Jesus that holy night. What joy and happiness we can experience when we reflect on the meaning and significance of this gift and embrace it with faith-filled hearts!

For Second and Third Graders

Ask the children to remember times when they have had special meals with their family or friends. Let them share their stories. Tell them some of your favorites. Talk together about what made the times happy. Review and explain the words the priest says to the assembly at this part of the Mass. Repeat the line "Blessed are those called to the supper of the Lamb." Explain how Mass may not look like those meals they described, but we are blessed because Christ is truly present. This is what the priest means when he says those words to us. Talk together about what they can do to make their family meals a happy time for everyone.

- Have your students do the activity on page 28 in the children's edition.

For Fourth and Fifth Graders

Brainstorm with the children ways the Eucharist is like a family meal. Then review how the Last Supper was a meal when the Eucharist was instituted. Together read the words the priest says at this point in the Mass, emphasizing the second sentence. Discuss with them why those who receive Communion have reason to feel blessed. Ask them how they can make their family meals more like the Eucharist; e.g., eating together, praying together beforehand, treating the others at the family with respect. Write down the suggestions for all to see. Give them quiet time to decide what they will take home in their hearts and carry out.

During the breaking of the bread we sing or say:

Lamb of God, you take away the sins of the world,
    have mercy on us.
Lamb of God, you take away the sins of the world,
    have mercy on us.
Lamb of God, you take away the sins of the world,
    grant us peace.

At the end of the Lamb of God we kneel.

Communion

The priest now invites us to come to the Lord's table and receive Holy Communion.

The priest says: *Behold the Lamb of God,*
behold him who takes away the sins of the world.
Blessed are those called to the supper of the Lamb.

We respond together with the priest:
Lord, I am not

_____

that you should enter under my roof,
but only _____ _____ _____
and my soul shall be healed.

ACTIVITY:

Read from the Gospel according to Matthew (8:3–13) to see where these words come from and who said them.

For Teachers and Catechists

Once again, during Holy Communion we have the opportunity to make an act of faith. We do this by saying, "Amen!" ("I believe it" or "So be it") when we receive the Body and Blood of Christ. So our response to the priest or other minister of Holy Communion should be said with a strong voice to show that we really do mean it—we really do believe that this is the Body of Christ and the Blood of Christ. Not only do we believe in this change of the bread and wine into the Body and Blood of Christ, but we also believe in the change that they can make in us. This faith, this sacrament, can help us be the person Christ wants us to become. Since the Second Vatican Council, we are again allowed to both "Take and eat" and "Take and drink," though we believe Christ is present in each of species equally. What a gift!

For Second and Third Graders

Let the children give you examples of what they eat and drink at a meal at home. Tell them the story of Jesus and the apostles eating together at a table. Then, with a hushed voice describe the point at which Jesus instituted Eucharist. Repeat what he said and what he did. Be sure they understand the connection with Eucharist today. Let them tell you what is different about the bread and wine when it is received at Mass. Tell them how it looks the same, but that because of our faith, we know it is the Body and Blood of Christ. On two sections of folded paper, let them illustrate both a meal at home and people receiving the Body and Blood of Christ at Mass.

For Fourth and Fifth Graders

Have parish or school hymnals available to the students. In pairs let them choose one of the hymns sung during Holy Communion. Let them read through the lyrics and share what they teach or say about Eucharist. List some of the ideas for all to see. Proclaim 1 Corinthians 11:23–26, which relates the Last Supper, telling them to listen for what connections they can make with the lyrics they chose. Explain how fortunate we are today to be able to receive under both species, and the significance of our Amen as an act of faith. Let them choose a Communion Song to sing together.

After we have said these words, we join in the procession, singing joyfully as we go forward to the altar to receive the Body and Blood of Christ.

The minister of Holy Communion is the priest but it can also be the deacon or another member of the congregation.

The minister holds the Body of Christ before us and says: *The Body of Christ.*

We respond: *A _____* , and then we eat the host.

Another minister may give us the cup to drink, saying: *The Blood of Christ.*

Again we reply, *A _____.*

29

Prayer after Communion

For Teachers and Catechists

During Holy Communion we have three kinds of prayers. The first is while everyone is coming in procession to receive Holy Communion. At this time, we all pray in the words of the Communion Chant. Just as at a meal at home, we eat and drink individually, and yet we are eating together so we pay attention to the others at the table. At Mass, when everyone has "eaten" and "drunk," we have a time of silence when we bow our heads and pray alone. That is the second kind of prayer during Holy Communion. Thirdly, the priest invites us to stand and once again pray in community. This time, the priest says the prayer aloud for all of us, and again, we make the prayer our own by our Amen.

For Second and Third Graders

After you have talked with the children about the three kinds of prayer during Holy Communion, let the entire group role-play the actions of this part of the Mass. Use a familiar Communion Chant, stressing that we are praying when we sing. After those who have made their first Holy Communion have "received," let them bow their heads and do a little "guided meditation" for them to say in their hearts. For example, you might say: *Now we thank Christ for coming to us in Holy Communion. Say this silently in your own words. Now we tell him that we love him and tell him some of the good things we did this week. Now we ask him to be with us to remind us to do good things in the coming week.*

For Fourth and Fifth Graders

After you have talked about the three kinds of prayer during Holy Communion, let the entire group role-play the actions of this part of Mass. Use a familiar Communion Chant, stressing that liturgical songs are prayers set to music. After all have "received," let them bow their heads and do a brief "guided meditation." For example, you might say: *In your own words, thank Christ for coming to you in communion. (Pause). Share with Christ some of the good things you did this week and ask him to help you do things this week that he would do in your place.*

- Have your students do the activity on page 30 in the children's edition.

We then return to our place, singing still, and when we are at our seat we pray silently and specially with Jesus in our hearts.

> ### ACTIVITY:
>
> Write a prayer to Jesus.
>
> Dear Jesus, _____
> _____
> _____
> _____

Prayer after Communion

After the procession to receive Holy Communion has finished and the singing has ended, we pray the Prayer after Communion. This prayer begins when the priest says: *Let us pray.*

At this signal we all stand, and after a short silence the priest then prays the prayer.

We respond: *A _____ .*

④ Concluding Rites

For Teachers and Catechists

Refer back to the beginning of Mass (see page 1 under "For Teachers and Catechists"). We begin and end Mass with the Sign of the Cross, our traditional Trinitarian way to begin and end all prayers. In this case, the priest doesn't make the Sign of the Cross on himself but makes it over us in a blessing. We, however, make the Sign of the Cross on ourselves as a response of receiving this blessing and as our closing prayer. There may be a longer and more elaborate blessing as the text indicates, but it will always end with this sign. In the book that the celebrant uses for Mass (*The Roman Missal*), you will find additional longer blessings. Read over some of these to be able to share them with the older children and help them listen for those on special occasions.

Concluding Rites

The Mass now comes to a close and we prepare to leave the church. We have been refreshed and are now keen to live like sisters and brothers of Christ, following his example and living his teachings.

The Blessing

After any announcements the priest gives a blessing.

Priest: *The Lord be with you.*

We respond: _____ _____

_____ _____ .

Priest: *May almighty God bless you,*
the Father, and the Son,
and the Holy Spirit.

We respond: A_____ .

Sometimes, on special days like Easter Sunday, the priest may give a longer and more solemn blessing. Here is an example.

Priest: *The Lord be with you.*

We respond: _____ _____

_____ _____ .

For Second and Third Graders

Have the children look again at the page with the Sign of the Cross at the beginning of Mass. Let them tell you how much they remember from that session. Fill in any information they don't recall. Stress that just as we began the Eucharistic celebration with this prayer, now we will end it the same way. Explain the difference in how the priest makes this sign on himself at the beginning of Mass and over us at the end of Mass. Divide into groups with each group demonstrating just one part of the Sign of the Cross. For example, one group takes "In the name of the Father . . . ." Another group takes ". . . and of the Son. . . ." and the final group takes ". . . and of the Holy Spirit." Have them stand in sequence and say and sign each part. Then let the entire group make the Sign of the Cross, saying the words together.

For Fourth and Fifth Graders

Talk again with the children about the Sign of the Cross and its theological significance, as well as the traditional way to begin and end prayer including the Mass. Have them read and compare the longer version in their text. If possible, have the priest come and share some of the variations with the class, concluding with him giving the group his blessing.

For Teachers and Catechists

Eucharist, like the Gospel itself is a "two-edged sword." It both comforts us and challenges us. We come to Eucharist to be fed and fed. We are fed with the word of the Lord in the scriptures and the Body and Blood of Christ in the consecrated bread and wine. Eucharist also challenges us by reminding us that we are to be Christ in our corner of the world today. We are here to care for others. We are not alone in doing Christ's work. Rather, he both told us to care for one another, and he still remains with us every minute of our lives. He is with us as we are like the good Samaritan, caring for someone in need. He is with us as we serve others by living out the Beatitudes. We are fed and strengthened, and we are to do the same for others. This is what is meant by the words "Go and announce the Gospel of the Lord." As Christ told us, whatever you do to others, you do to me. What a privilege!

For Second and Third Graders

Review this part of Mass with the children, helping them to learn to say their response, "Thanks be to God!" enthusiastically. Let them think of the many reasons we have to say this thank-you. Explore different ways they can show thanks by being of service. Together make a list of concrete things they might do for other people. Let them choose two or three things from the list that they want to do. Have each child make a page that lists his other choices: "To say thank-you to God, I am going to _____." When all have finished, let them share their choices.

For Fourth and Fifth Graders

Let the students explain this part of the liturgy from their experience and from the text. Focus on the final prayer of the deacon or priest and discuss its meaning together. Emphasize our special call to service for our family and our community. Together, brainstorm how the parish community takes care of each other. Together, list ways they can be of service at home and within the parish. Play quiet music and allow time for them to study both lists and make a resolution in their hearts what they want to do this week. Conclude with a familiar closing song from your parish or school hymnal.

For Teachers and Catechists

Eucharist means "thanksgiving" in Greek. *Mass* comes from the Latin verb meaning, "to send forth." Both of these themes are richly integrated into all that we do and say in the liturgy. We come with much to be thankful for, and we leave with even more reason to go forth and do the will of the Lord. We are part of the larger community of the parish, the global church, and the community of all God's people on earth. As the world grows smaller, today we are even more aware of the suffering of all humanity. We are also more able to connect with people around the world in ways that we can be of service—by what we do, what we give, and always, by our prayers for them.

Priest: *May God, who by the Resurrection of his Only Begotten Son was pleased to confer on you the gift of redemption and of adoption, give you gladness by his blessing.*

We respond: *A_____ .*

Priest: *May he, by whose redeeming work you have received the gift of everlasting freedom, make you heirs to an eternal inheritance.*

We respond: *A_____ .*

Priest: *And may you, who have already risen with Christ in Baptism through faith, by living in a right manner on this earth, be united with him in the homeland of heaven.*

We respond: *A_____ .*

Priest: *And may the blessing of almighty God, the Father, and the Son, and the Holy Spirit, come down on you and remain with you for ever.*

We respond: *A_____ .*

As the priest gives the blessing, we follow the custom and make the Sign of the Cross.

For Second and Third Graders

Spend time together with the children paging through the children's book. Ask the students questions about significant parts of the Mass and remind them of the importance of each. Use this time as both a review and celebration. Let them tell you of their favorite part of Mass or the best thing they learned. Conclude with a little party with refreshments to celebrate the wonderful gift of Eucharist that Christ gave us.

For Fourth and Fifth Graders

Remind the students that while we have thought about being of service to those near us, we are also called to serve people outside our community and even outside our country. Bring several newspapers and let them look for examples of such people who need help. In small groups, brainstorm ways people here might be of help. Share their ideas with the larger group. Be sure to connect the importance of service with the meaning of Mass. Assign certain parts of Mass to each student. Allow them time to look over the children's book. Go through Mass in its proper sequence, and then have them take turns giving an oral quiz to each other to see how much they remember.

• Have your students do the activity on page 33 in the children's edition.

ACTIVITY:

When Mass has finished, what are some of the things I can do to share the love I have received from Jesus?

(Write your answers below, and share them with others.)

33

For Teachers and Catechists

In the 2007 papal exhortation *Sacramentum Caritatis*, Pope Benedict XVI speaks of the importance of the words in the Final Dismissal. He explains that what is said in the dismissal should link the relationship between the Mass and our mission in the world. When we leave Mass, we are being sent into the world to proclaim the Gospel. In other words, we are being dispatched to our mission of bringing Christ to those we meet in our homes, our neighborhoods, our schools, and our workplaces. Wherever we are, we have a chance to show others the face of Christ. We do this by the way we treat and speak to those we encounter.

Pope Benedict noted that it would be beneficial to provide new texts for the dismissal that would make the connection between Mass and our mission clear. Consider the dismissal "Go and announce the Gospel of the Lord." How does that speak to you? Does that make you realize that your life should reflect the Good News of Jesus Christ? Consider, too, the dismissal "Go in peace, glorifying the Lord by your life." Do you take seriously these words that your life should lend glory to God?

For Second and Third Graders

Have the children gather in small groups. Each group can decide which dismissal to draw or enact. Ask them to consider how they would portray one of the dismissals. First discuss each of the dismissals. Explain that "Go forth, the Mass is ended" means that we are sent into the world to do the work of Christ. Note that "Go and announce the Gospel of the Lord" means more than telling people about the reading of the day. Discuss with them that the word *Gospel* means "good news." What does this "good news" mean to them? How do they tell it to others? Do they live differently because of the "good news"?

For Fourth and Fifth Graders

Ask the students to choose to read either the story of the Samaritan woman at the well (John 4:5–42) or the story of the angel appearing to the women at the tomb (Matthew 28:1–10).

After the students have read the story, invite them to discuss the joy with which the "good news" was announced. The Samaritan woman apparently could not wait to tell the people in the town about the Lord. The townspeople believed because "of the word of the woman who testified." The angel told the women at the tomb to quickly tell the disciples that Jesus was raised. They "ran to announce this to the disciples." In the story, Jesus meets the women and says, "Go tell my brothers to go to Galilee . . . ." Discuss with the children how the words *announce* and *go* are in the dismissal and in the words of the Gospel. Invite the students to discuss what it means to announce the Gospel.

Final Dismissal

The deacon or priest leads the final prayer: He may say one of the four options:

> Go forth the Mass is ended.
> Go and announce the Gospel of the Lord.
> Go in peace, glorifying the Lord by
>   your life.
> Go in peace.

We respond: _____ ____ ____ _____ .

The Mass is now finished, and we sometimes have a song and a procession to bring everything to a close. As we leave we begin again to live as Jesus taught us, especially to bring love and peace to everyone we meet.

Answer Key

Here is the answer key for the "fill-in-the-blank" questions in the children's edition. Review the answers with your students.

CHAPTER 1:   INTRODUCTORY RITES

Page 4:   **The Sign of the Cross**

In the name of the **Father**, and of the **Son**, and of the **Holy Spirit.**

We respond: **Amen.**

Page 4:   **The Greeting**

We respond: And **with your spirit.**

Page 6:   **The Penitential Act**

We respond with **Christ, have mercy.**

Page 7:   **The Collect**

We respond by saying: **Amen.**

CHAPTER 2: THE LITURGY OF THE WORD

Page 9:   **The Liturgy of the Word**

The readings are in a book called the **Lectionary.**

Page 10:   **The First Reading**

We reply: **Thanks be to God.**

Page 10:   **The Second Reading**

Again the reading finishes when the reader says: **The word of the Lord.**

Page 11:   **The Gospel**

The names of the four evangelists are **Matthew, Mark, Luke, and John.**

We know the Gospel is special because we often sing the word **Alleluia.**

We also know it is special because we sometimes include the Gospel in a book called the **Book of the Gospels.**

Deacon or priest: A reading from the holy Gospel according to **Matthew** or **Mark** or **Luke** or **John.**

We respond: **Glory to you, O Lord.**

Page 12:   **The Gospel**

We reply: **Praise to you, Lord Jesus Christ.**

CHAPTER 3: THE LITURGY OF THE EUCHARIST

Page 18: **Presentation and Preparation of the Gifts**

We respond: **Blessed be God for ever.**

Page 19: **Presentation and Preparation of the Gifts**

We respond: **Blessed be God for ever.**

We respond by saying: **Amen.**

Page 23: **Memorial Acclamation**

We proclaim your **Death**, O Lord,
and profess your **Resurrection**
until you come again.

or
When we **eat** this Bread and **drink** this Cup,
we **proclaim** your Death, O Lord,
until you come again

or
Save us, Savior of the **world**,
for by your Cross and **Resurrection**,
you have set us free.

Page 24: **The Doxology (Amen)**

We bring the prayer to an end when we sing: **Amen.**

Page 25: **The Lord's Prayer**

We respond: For the kingdom, the **power,** and **the glory** are yours, **now** and **for ever.**

Page 26: **Sign of Peace**

We respond: **Amen.**

We reply: **And with your spirit.**

We do this by shaking **hands** and saying, "Peace be **with you**" to those who are near us.

Page 28: **Communion**

We respond together with the priest:

Lord, I am not **worthy**
that you should enter under my roof,
but only **say the word**
and my soul shall be **healed.**

Page 29: **Communion**

We respond: **Amen.**

Again we reply: **Amen.**

Page 30: **Prayer after Communion**

We respond: **Amen.**

CHAPTER 4: CONCLUDING RITES

Page 31: **The Blessing**

We respond: **And with your spirit.**

We respond: **Amen.**

We respond: **And with your spirit.**

We respond: **Amen.**

Page 32: **The Blessing**

We respond: **Amen.**

We respond: **Amen.**

We respond: **Amen.**

Page 34: **Final Dismissal**

We respond: **Thanks be to God.**

The Authors

Dr. Gerard Moore has taught liturgy for many years, and has served as a consultant to the International Commission on English in the Liturgy. He is currently the Director of Research for the Sydney College of Divinity.

Jean Marie Hiesberger is a religious educator and ministry leadership trainer who has taught in graduate programs at six universities and given keynote addresses and workshops throughout the United States, Canada, Italy, Germany, and Jamaica. She is the author of numerous articles, and has written or contributed to over thirty books and catechetical programs. She is listed in *Who's Who in Religion* and *Who's Who in American Women* and has been interviewed by Ladies' Home Journal and the Los Angeles Times. Her book *Fostering Leadership Skills in the Parish* won a Catholic Press Association award and she is the recipient of the National Association for Lay Ministry *Gaudium Et Spes* Award.

The Illustrators

Jim Burrows provided the cover art. Jim shares the Good News of the Gospel through a variety of media. He creates a weekly Lectionary-based cartoon series for church bulletins and diocesan newspapers. Jim is enrolled in the master's degree program in pastoral studies at Loyola University New Orleans and is in formation for the permanent diaconate for the Diocese of Monterey. He is a certified catechist at Mission San Luis Obispo in California.

Sister Dorothy Woodward, RSJ, is responsible for the interior art. She has wide experience in Catholic education, and a special interest in liturgical art and design.

Resources

To learn more about Mass, visit www.LTP.org for various resources for children, parents, teachers, and parishes.